ReSurfacing®

Techniques for Exploring Consciousness

by Harry Palmer

Avatar®

ReSurfacing is dedicated to the global network of Avatars, Masters and Wizards, as well as other white-light warriors, who inwardly and outwardly are contributing to the creation of an enlightened planetary civilization.

Cover Art by
Jim Becker

Editorial Assistance
Kayt Kennedy
Avra Honey-Smith
Miken Chappell

All our love to the people who contributed to the creation of this workbook.

Published by

Star's Edge® International
237 North Westmonte Drive
Altamonte Springs, Florida 32714
USA

Avatar®, ReSurfacing® and Star's Edge International® are registered
service marks licensed to Star's Edge, Inc.

ISBN: 0-9626874-9-9

TABLE OF CONTENTS

Part IV You

Part V The Next Step

Part VI Index

LIST OF EXERCISES

The miracle is not that there is
life within the universe;

the miracle is that there is a
universe within life.

The miracle is not that
consciousness evolved out of
the universe;

the miracle is that the universe
evolved out of consciousness.

The miracle is not that the
here/now contains a you;

the miracle is that you contain
a here/now.

Oh, my ancient companions,
wake from your long sleep.

There is so much I have to
show you.

Translarian Message*

* From the Translarian Record, an
unfinished manuscript by the author,
which chronicles the spread of sentient
life throughout the Milky Way galaxy.

FOUR APPROACHES TO THE RESURFACING WORKBOOK

1. As a personal workbook

For several years, people have been asking me for an inexpensive Avatar workbook of self-development materials that they could work on in their spare time in the privacy of their own home. Here it is. Start with the Orientation section on page 1 and continue through to the Debrief exercise on page 133. Be understanding with yourself, and let me know how you make out.

2. As a text for Section I of The Avatar® Course

In 1988 we discovered that people required a certain amount of preliminary information about Avatar before making a commitment to do the course. We designed a checklist of assignments and exercises that produced insights into what Avatar was about and where it led. This checklist became Section I of The Avatar Course and is used today by Avatar Masters as a foundation for Sections II and III. If you are doing the Section I checklist with a Master, follow the assignments and exercises in the order of the checklist.

3. As reference course materials for ReSurfacing® workshops

Some people prefer to approach Avatar in an intensive workshop lasting for two or three days. These are presented by Avatar Masters in informal small group workshops that permit lots of interaction and sharing. If you are doing a ReSurfacing® workshop, the Master will direct the order in which you do the exercises and read the selections.

4. As a reference and exercise source for self-evolvement classes and study groups

You are welcome to use the ReSurfacing workbook in its original form (no excerpts or photocopies) as part of any class.

PART I

ORIENTATION

The **ReSurfacing**
workbook is an
instructional log for
explorers traveling
beyond the realm of
familiar consciousness.

It contains the exercises
and study materials of
Section I of The
Avatar® Course.

ORIENTATION

ReSurfacing refers to the action of disentangling yourself from old creations and rising back into awareness. It is a process, paralleling nature, of revealing yourself to yourself. The rewards are new insights and realizations about how your life works — or why it doesn't work.

ReSurfacing is an expedition into consciousness that you personalize according to your own needs. How far you go is a matter for you to determine. There will be no effort to indoctrinate you with any belief or truth. What you believe is what you believe, and the truth you discover is your truth.

As you proceed, you will become aware of your own creative power. It will surprise and amaze you. Should you choose to follow this power to its source, you will find a measureless sea of awareness extending beyond time, consciousness, and creation. Ancient companions wait for you (t)here.

The power of the Avatar materials comes from the same fundamental principles that govern creation. The first principle, the one that may take some getting used to, is that both the physical universe and personal consciousness arise from a definitionless, adimensional presence, which the Avatar materials refer to as awareness, life source, or pure beingness. Every effort to measure, define or describe this presence is ultimately a failure, still…

Even a few minutes spent on the exercises in this book can have a profound effect on your life.

All of the struggles between self and the world come from an ignorance of this first principle. At first the separation between your consciousness and the universe seems an insurmountable abyss, an evilly brilliant trap. Then the technology of Avatar appears, and you begin to get your first vague experience of something that underlies and connects the mental and the physical, a unifying presence—a definition-less, adimensional awareness.

The materials of Sections II and III of Avatar develop the inherent abilities of the transcendent self to experience and restructure reality deliberately.

The exercises that follow will bring forth a you that transcends all the ideas you've imagined yourself or the world to be. This moment of transcendence, or resurfacing, is a glimpse into the realm opened by the Avatar materials. Welcome home.

The Structure of Consciousness

ReSurfacing is a new approach to some very old puzzles: who am I, why am I here, where am I going? With *ReSurfacing* you find the answers to these questions by exploring the underlying structure of your conscious-ness—beliefs.

✪ Beliefs are the thoughtforms through which you create, interpret and interact with reality.

Study anything thoroughly enough, and you'll be exploring beliefs.

✪ Beliefs create separation between self and the universe (e.g., This is me. That is that.).

✪ Beliefs interpret and, within certain self-deter-mined parameters, create the experiences that confirm the truth of what is believed (e.g., Life is hard.).

- Beliefs create a cause-and-effect/effect-and-cause relationship between self and the physical universe (e.g., Because I believe…; I believe because…).

- By managing beliefs you have the power to restructure consciousness and create new realities.

ReSurfacing is Experiential

There are word lessons and there are world lessons. A word lesson is an effort to convey an experience via spoken or written symbols. A word lesson can be informative or enjoyable or inspiring. A word lesson is an expression of someone's belief. A word lesson can be a very nice thing, but it should not be confused with a world lesson.

experiential *personal involvement in or observation of* events as they occur

A world lesson is something that you live through. It's something you encounter and deal with in life. And from the world lesson you emerge changed, more experienced, wiser. A world lesson is an experience. It does not require translation into symbols or sounds for you to remember it. It becomes part of what you know, of how you define yourself to yourself. A word lesson seldom has this impact.

A world lesson becomes a word lesson as soon as it is expressed. *What you know becomes a belief as soon as it is expressed.* A word lesson can convey descriptions and instructions, but as far as experience, it is a pale substitute.

Consider: What is the difference between eating an apple and studying what an apple tastes like?

Your study of *ReSurfacing* begins as a word lesson describing exercises and conveying instructions, but as you participate, it changes to a world lesson. The word lessons of *ReSurfacing* are insignificant compared to the world lessons you create by your participation.

The World Lessons

Use *ReSurfacing* to gain experiential knowing in regard to the following questions:

☆ Who am I?

☆ What determines my experience?

☆ What determines my belief?

☆ What is a self?

☆ What is real?

☆ What is shared reality?

☆ What is true?

Two Points to Remember

First, the most important discoveries you will make are the beliefs and belief systems contained in your own consciousness. Some of these may be immediately apparent while others are transparent, meaning that you perceive and act through them without realizing it. These transparent beliefs affect the understanding and workability of everything else. For example, if you perceive and act through the belief that you can't improve yourself, that belief will sabotage any attempt you make to improve. To be safe, be as vulnerable as you can be; leave open the possibility that your certain truth might actually be a transparent belief.

Second, the written materials are meant as guides for you to use. Use them in harmony with your own integrity. They are intended to indicate direction and possibility rather than to present dogma or law. Understanding the concepts is more important than memorizing the words. Nothing should be construed, in any sense, as constituting a belief you must or should subscribe to forever.

The Difficulty with Simplicity

People who have completed this adventure have commented that the most difficult thing to accept is the utter simplicity of the insights. Perhaps this is because many of us carry along the idea (transparent belief) that anything powerful and liberating must also be complex.

As it turns out, something is complex only to the degree that it does not fit with what you already believe. So occasionally on this ascent, like a diver who has been down for a long time, you should make a decompression stop and take time to consider, integrate, and express your feelings and observations. These pauses and the journal entries you make are essential steps for growth and learning. As long as your insights are becoming simpler and more experiential, you're on the right track.

If the work becomes intellectual and abstract, slow down and allow yourself time to relax. If you flounder on an unfamiliar word, feel blank, or if something doesn't make sense, take it apart slowly, use a dictionary, or call upon an Avatar Master. Some words used in the Avatar materials have specialized meanings. These are found in **bold** in the sidebars.

Spend whatever time you need to gain an understanding of the words and ideas you encounter. Demonstrating concepts with familiar objects—pens, pencils, coins, keys, etc.—can accelerate comprehension.

Finally, go beyond understanding the words. Seek an experiential clarity of what is encountered. Bring it into your tent and try it on. If you've been studying about the taste of apples, go eat an apple.

Breaking the Surface

*Student:
How do I know when
I'm experiencing?*

*Avatar:
Be with exactly what
you are feeling without
using any pictures or
words. There, you are
experiencing!*

The exercises will lead you to an experience of your personal study materials. These are the motives and principles that govern your existence. They are as unique as your fingerprints. Discovering them will take you to new places and new viewpoints that will dramatically broaden your comprehension of existence.

When you combine the word lessons with world lessons, you achieve a moment of realization: *so that's how it works!* Realizations increase your ability to broadly and creatively apply what you know. Realizations compound. The more realizations you have, the simpler and clearer all things become. Realizations are the stuff of real wisdom.

If you suspect that you are engaging the materials only on an intellectual or a reflective basis, *do the exercises.* Doing the exercises will help you to achieve a deeper appreciation than thought alone can reach.

For the few hours of this adventure, put your outer cares aside and devote yourself to discovering yourself and resurfacing into the limitless potential that awaits. Prepare to experience your creation of consciousness and the physical universe in all its wonder.

The Avatar Master Course, Gardone Riviera, Italy

PERSONALITY PROFILE

ReSurfacing is formatted with spaces for you to write your answers and observations. A study of these responses will give you an overview of the creation you regard as self. This is generally a more expansive vista than you expect. Later you can use your responses to verify the results that the exercises have had upon your life.

If there is something you would rather not respond to, just go on to the next question or exercise. There are no standards you must live up to, no right or wrong answers. If you are uncomfortable writing in the book, even with a pencil, it is still recommended that you record your responses somewhere. Consciousness can be a maze, and mapping as you go can keep you from visiting dead ends repeatedly.

profile *a view of anything in contour; outline*

If a question calls for a spontaneous answer, take your first impression as the answer. These answers are written down exactly as you think of them. If they don't always make sense, that's all right. Your responses are pieces to a larger puzzle that will reveal unknown areas of your consciousness. When the puzzle pieces come together, you will understand how these unfamiliar areas are influencing you.

Exercise 1

PERSONALITY PROFILE

The first step in handling a confusion is to call up (or re-create) the existing blueprint. This gives reference points against which things can be measured and organized.

OBJECTIVE:

To construct a blueprint of how you currently regard self.

EXPECTED RESULTS:

Insights, improved well-being, recovery of self-determinism.

INSTRUCTIONS:

Unless otherwise noted, the following questions should be answered in detail. (Some will call for spontaneous answers.) Please do not feel self-conscious or become self-judgmental about what you write or how you say anything. There is no model against which your answers are judged, so there is no need to consult any model as you write them. If something evokes more emotion (grief, fear, guilt, anger, etc.) than you wish to experience, note it as a sensitive area and go on to the next question. You'll return and handle sensitive areas in a future exercise.

If you don't know the answer to something, you may either guess or write "don't know." Enjoy the questions. Be with them and treat them as if they were all you need to do.

EX 1
EX 2
EX 3
EX 4
EX 5
EX 6
EX 7
EX 8
EX 9
EX 10
EX 11
EX 12
EX 13
EX 14
EX 15
EX 16
EX 17
EX 18
EX 19
EX 20
EX 21
EX 22
EX 23
EX 24
EX 25
EX 26
EX 27
EX 28
EX 29
EX 30

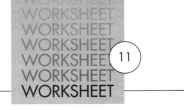

PERSONALITY PROFILE

Today's date:_____

Name: _____

Address: _____

_____

Country, zip/postal code: _____

Telephone:_____ Date of birth: _____

A. Give a spontaneous answer to the following:

Life is_____

Life is_____

Life is_____

Life is_____

Life is_____

Life is_____

exercise continues

PERSONALITY PROFILE

B. Record of *formal* education (what studied, how long, result):

           Subject   *Duration*   *What happened?*

1._____

_____

_____

2._____

_____

_____

3._____

_____

_____

4._____

_____

_____

C. Give a spontaneous answer for each subject you listed:
   Who motivated you to study this?

1._____

_____

2._____

_____

PERSONALITY PROFILE

WORKSHEET
WORKSHEET
WORKSHEET
WORKSHEET
WORKSHEE 13
WORKSHEET
WORKSHEET

3._____

_____

4._____

_____

D. Record of *informal* education (what studied, how long, result):

	Subject	Duration	What happened?

1._____

2._____

3._____

4._____

exercise continues

Subject	Duration	What happened?

5._____

_____

_____

E. Give a spontaneous answer for each subject you listed:
   What was your purpose in studying this?

1._____

2._____

3._____

4._____

5._____

F. Skills you have acquired that you are proud of:

1._____

2._____

3._____

4._____

5._____

PERSONALITY PROFILE

WORKSHEET
WORKSHEET
WORKSHEET
WORKSHEET
WORKSHEE 15
WORKSHEET
WORKSHEET

G. Give a spontaneous answer for each acquired skill above:
   Who would be surprised?

1._____

2._____

3._____

4._____

5._____

H. Accomplishments you are proud of:

1._____

2._____

3._____

4._____

5._____

I. Give a spontaneous answer for each accomplishment above:
   Who was wrong about you?

1._____

2._____

3._____

4._____

5._____

exercise continues

J. What is your current means of livelihood, and how did you come to be
so employed?

_____

_____

_____

_____

_____

K. Speculate: What would you do for a livelihood if given the opportunity?

_____

_____

_____

_____

_____

L. What is your marital history and the current status of each relationship?

_____

_____

_____

_____

_____

PERSONALITY PROFILE

WORKSHEET
WORKSHEET
WORKSHEET
WORKSHEET
WORKSHEET
WORKSHEET
WORKSHEET

17

M. Speculate on the ideal relationship:

_____

_____

_____

_____

_____

N. List the names of your children and the current status of your relationship with each.

　　　Child's name　　　*Status of relationship*

_____

_____

_____

_____

O. Give a spontaneous answer: What purposes are you attempting to forward through each of your offspring?

_____

_____

_____

_____

exercise continues

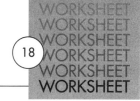

P. List the names of your parents (or surrogates) and the current status of your relationship with each.

Parent's name   *Status of relationship*

_____

_____

_____

_____

Q. Speculate on your father's life purpose:

_____

_____

_____

_____

R. Speculate on your mother's life purpose:

_____

_____

_____

_____

S. Speculate on a goal that would combine your father's life purpose and your mother's life purpose:

_____

_____

_____

_____

_____

T. Beginning with grade school, list the major periods of your life (childhood home, moved to Chicago, etc.):

1._____

2._____

3._____

4._____

5._____

6._____

7._____

exercise continues

U. Give a spontaneous answer for each of the above:
   Who did you think about most during that period?

1._____

2._____

3._____

4._____

5._____

6._____

7._____

V. What period(s) of your life do you like best? Why?

_____

_____

_____

_____

W. What period(s) of your life do you like least? Why?

_____

_____

_____

_____

WORKSHEET
WORKSHEET
WORKSHEET
WORKSHEET
WORKSHEE 21
WORKSHEE
WORKSHEET

X. What aspects of your current creation of self do you like least?

1._____

2._____

3._____

4._____

5._____

Y. Give a spontaneous answer for each of the above:
   Who does that resemble?

1._____

2._____

3._____

4._____

5._____

Z. What aspects of your current creation of self do you like best?

1._____

2._____

3._____

4._____

5._____

exercise continues

AA. Give a spontaneous answer for each of the above:
Who does that resemble?

1._____

2._____

3._____

4._____

5._____

BB. List the names of people you consider most supportive of you:

1._____

2._____

3._____

4._____

5._____

CC. List the names of people you consider unsupportive of you:

1._____

2._____

3._____

4._____

5._____

WORKSHEET
WORKSHEET
WORKSHEET
WORKSHEET
WORKSHEET 23
WORKSHEET
WORKSHEET

DD. List the names of people who rely on your support:

1._____

2._____

3._____

4._____

5._____

EE. List the names of people who have abused your support:

1._____

2._____

3._____

4._____

5._____

FF. List aspects of your physical health that currently concern you:

1._____

2._____

3._____

4._____

5._____

exercise continues

WORKSHEET (watermark)

GG. List your most frequent worries and speculate on what might eliminate them.

1._____

_____

2._____

_____

3._____

_____

4._____

_____

5._____

_____

HH. What are your greatest strengths?

1._____

2._____

3._____

4._____

5._____

II. What are your principle desires?

1._____

2._____

3._____

4._____

5._____

JJ. If you were to receive an award, what would you like it to be for?

_____

_____

_____

_____

KK. If you were to receive an award, who would you like to have know about it?

1._____

2._____

3._____

4._____

5._____

exercise continues

LL. About what do you exaggerate?

1._____

2._____

3._____

4._____

5._____

MM. What things do you consider most important?

1._____

2._____

3._____

4._____

5._____

NN. What hurts you most?

1._____

2._____

3._____

4._____

5._____

PERSONALITY PROFILE

WORKSHEET
WORKSHEET
WORKSHEET
WORKSHEET
WORKSHEET 27
WORKSHEET
WORKSHEET

OO. Give a spontaneous answer for each of the above:
Realistically, how could that be repaired?

1._____

2._____

3._____

4._____

5._____

PP. Who would it please you to have apologize?

1._____

2._____

3._____

4._____

5._____

QQ. What would it take to convince you that you had succeeded?

_____

_____

_____

_____

_____

exercise continues

PERSONALITY PROFILE

RR. In filling out this profile, whose names showed up the most?

1._____

2._____

3._____

4._____

5._____

SS. For each of the above, list five differences between you and that person:

1._____

2._____

3._____

4._____

5._____

1._____

2._____

3._____

4._____

5._____

PERSONALITY PROFILE

WORKSHEET
WORKSHEET
WORKSHEET
WORKSHEET
WORKSHEET
WORKSHEET
WORKSHEET

(29)

1. _____

2. _____

3. _____

4. _____

5. _____

1. _____

2. _____

3. _____

4. _____

5. _____

1. _____

2. _____

3. _____

4. _____

5. _____

exercise continues

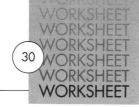
TT. If you could re-create yourself within your realistic limitations, what would you be like? Details please.

_____

_____

_____

_____

_____

_____

_____

_____

_____

_____

_____

_____

_____

_____

_____

_____

PART II

ATTENTION

Exercises that may be done solo

Exercises that may be done with a companion

Exercises that may be done as a group

Questions for contemplation or group discussion

*The word lessons of **ReSurfacing** are edited excerpts from lectures given by Harry Palmer between 1987 and 1992.*

WILL

will *the power of making a reasoned choice or decision or of controlling one's own actions*

Under the guise of socializing the individual, schools and governments discourage willful behavior. Willfulness is equated with stubbornness or obstinacy.

willful *said or done deliberately or intentionally*

So from disuse, the individual's will falls into a stupor and is kept sedated by stressful indoctrination. Awakening is discouraged by regulations that threaten painful consequences for mistakes. Personal responsibility is associated with blame and replaced by abstract ideas about right, which serve as justification for any action, no matter how selfish, immoral, or cruel.

indoctrinate *to fill someone with beliefs*

Methods of indoctrination have been developed into highly effective technologies over the last ten millenniums. The individual has become a puppet of ill-conceived lessons of long-dead pedagogues. As a result, the individual's will is in a very deep slumber. Accompanying this decline in the omnipotence of the will is an increasing concern with personal needs and gratifications. Awareness becomes spirits, minds, and/or bodies.

power *in general, such an absence of external restriction and limitation that it depends only upon the inward determination of the subject whether or not it will act*

omnipotent *having unlimited power or authority*

Low will power creates an addiction to directions, which is fed by truth-saying gurus, perpetuated by sign painters and validated by courts. Personal responsibility is deposed without fuss by uniform codes of law. Freedom is replaced by governmentally managed choices (e.g., You are free to pay your taxes by check or cash.).

For some, just encountering the idea of living deliberately begins to reawaken the will. Others are going to sleep through to the grave.

The ones who wake up look around and are amazed at the sleepwalker existence from which they have just emerged. The realization "I decide" frees them from their addiction to answers. Some awake so ashamed of their irresponsible behaviors that they become rebellious against all authority. Some even attack the source of their awakening.

A harmonic of this rebellious awakening is seen during late adolescence when inexperienced youths test their power of will over the smallest matters. Providing they escape complete indoctrination, responsibility matures and catches up with the will. They realize: the proper use of will power is not conquest and subjugation, but the disciplined control of one's own attention.

Freedom is a measure of the number of decisions a person makes. As long as there is more pleasure than pain connected with making decisions, a person desires more freedom and less indoctrination. When it is reversed, and there is more pain than pleasure connected with making decisions, a person desires less freedom and welcomes indoctrination.

Exercise 2

AWAKENING THE WILL

EX 1
EX 2
EX 3
EX 4
EX 5
EX 6
EX 7
EX 8
EX 9
EX 10
EX 11
EX 12
EX 13
EX 14
EX 15
EX 16
EX 17
EX 18
EX 19
EX 20
EX 21
EX 22
EX 23
EX 24
EX 25
EX 26
EX 27
EX 28
EX 29
EX 30

The will awakens slowly from sleep. At first it feels overwhelmed by the turbulence of thoughts that buffet it. Its initial attitude is: "Just tell me what you want, and I'll do it."

OBJECTIVE:

To strengthen the will by describing objects.

EXPECTED RESULTS:

Insights, calming, increased awareness.

INSTRUCTIONS:

Take a walk, notice something, and decide how you would describe it. Continue, noticing different objects.

GROUP VARIATION:

The group leader passes out cards that have the names of common objects. Without mentioning the object's name, each student describes what it feels like to be the object, and from the description the group tries to identify the object described. (Additional rules on how to play, score, etc., can be adopted by group agreement.)

Exercise 3

DISCIPLINING ATTENTION

OBJECTIVE:
To place the control of attention under the will.

EXPECTED RESULTS:
Increased sense of personal stability and power.

INSTRUCTIONS 1
Pick a stationary object, and direct your attention to it (examine it) for a period of two minutes. Any time your attention wanders, bring it back.

The exercise can be done in a group or with a coach who starts and ends the two-minute intervals. If after several tries you still have trouble with this step, return to Exercise 2.

Example:
Pick an object. Start.
(Two minutes later.)
That's it. Is your
attention still on that
object?

INSTRUCTIONS 2
Pick a mental image or memory, and direct your attention to it for a period of two minutes. The exercise can be done with a coach who starts and ends the two-minute interval. Any time your attention wanders, bring it back. Do whatever you have to do to keep the image from disappearing. If after several tries you still have trouble with this step of the exercise, return to examining stationary objects.

Example:
Pick a mental image.
(Have the person state it
briefly.) Start.
(Two minutes later.)
That's it. Is your
attention still on that
mental image?

Group Variation

SIMON SAYS

The group leader gives the group instructions: pat your head, stand up, shake your neighbor's hand, etc. The group members must follow only those instructions that are preceded by the phrase "Simon says"; otherwise they ignore the instructions. The person making the fewest mistakes in any round becomes the next leader.

The Avatar Master Course, Auckland, New Zealand

A self is an idea that awareness is availing itself of for the purpose of experiencing certain other ideas. It's the bubble from which you view other bubbles.

BEING AWARE WILL

Do we have any evidence at all for this definition-less awareness that I keep referring to?

It's outside of time; it's nonspatial; it's adimensional; it has no mass, no wavelength, no frequency—in short, it's unimaginable. Not that. Not that. Not that either.

It's beyond the parameters by which we determine whether something exists or not. Can you imagine something that's unimaginable? No! Put away your mind with all its labels and definitions. What evidence do we have for this definitionless awareness that remains when everything else is eliminated?

What's left? Only the eliminator.

When we understand this, all the things that it can't be described by are actually evidence of it. That. That. That too.

omnipresent *present in all places at the same time*

aware *watchful; vigilant; knowing*

will *the power to decide; to direct; to decree*

Feel what it feels like to be only, effortlessly, omnipresent aware will.

Aware will, pure consciousness, perfect balance, awake in the void.

Exercise 4

ACTING AS AWARE WILL

OBJECTIVE:

To place behavior under the control of the will.

EXPECTED RESULTS:

Recognition of your own programming and the ability to erase it.

INSTRUCTIONS

This is a very powerful exercise for awakening a higher awareness of self. You may make many tries before awareness becomes effortless. It is a gradient approach to self-discipline.

The exercise is done for five minutes each time and starts with the student sitting or standing quietly. (A coach is beneficial, but not required.)

After the start, the student may remain still or move anywhere he or she desires as long as he or she deliberately verbalizes (either vocally or mentally) the decision to move before moving. Any involuntary movements discovered should be: 1) stopped, 2) verbalized, and then 3) continued deliberately.

OPTION

The student can expand this exercise to a more advanced level by noticing the associations between involuntary behaviors and mental states.

Example: Student begins by standing.

(Decision): "I'm going to walk over to that wall."
   (Does so)

(Involuntary movement): Student catches self scratching the left side of head. *(Stops, notes to self a mental uncertainty)*

(Verbalizes decision): "I'm going to scratch the left side of my head." *(Does so until the mental uncertainty disassociates with the action)*

(Decision): "I'm going to stop scratching the left side of my head." *(Does so)*

(Decision): "I'm going to look out the window."
   (Does so).

Etc.

Exercise 5

THE WILL RULES ALL

All of the struggles between self and the world come from an ignorance of this principle: that consciousness and the universe arise from the same source. The will is a quality of this source and thus a bridge between the physical and the mental.

OBJECTIVE 1:

To show the effect that the will can have on mental state via a deliberate physical action.

INSTRUCTIONS:

Deliberately smile until you feel happy.

OBJECTIVE 2:

To show the effect that the will can have on physical action via a deliberate mental state.

INSTRUCTIONS:

Think to yourself "I'm happy" until you smile.

ATTENTION

The word attention is derived from two Latin words, *ad* meaning toward and *tendere* meaning stretch. When you put your attention on something, you stretch toward it. Look at something, and you stretch toward it. Once your curiosity is satisfied, your attention comes off whatever you were looking at, listening to, touching, etc., and moves to something else. Whoever or whatever attention is placed on becomes more real.

Reality is sustained by attention. Attention is the creating energy of both consciousness and the universe. It is the crossover region where thought changes to perception—the area where consciousness transforms into a reality that is apparent to the senses—and vice versa. This is where the physical manifests, where the word becomes universe. This is the star's edge.

Aware will directed through a viewpoint creates attention with the characteristics and intention of the viewpoint.

Attention manifests as both an energy (inquiring/creating) and as a subatomic particle (bearing information/creation). Attention energy (an inquiry/intention) can be controlled solely by your will, but once it becomes a particle (perception), its control requires both will and physical effort. If you wish to change something solely by the strength of your will, you must transform the attention particle (perception) back into an energy form (inquiring/creating); otherwise you're faced with rolling up your sleeves and exerting enough physical effort to move the particles around—a very primitive approach actually.

The function of will is to decide, place, shift, or remove attention.

Exercise 6

CONTROLLING ATTENTION

OBJECTIVE:

To increase your ability to control attention.

EXPECTED RESULTS:

Insights, improved well-being, recovery of self-determinism.

INSTRUCTIONS

To be read aloud to the group by the group leader, who pauses after each statement (approx. ten seconds) until the group has complied.

1. Look at the front wall, and find something you haven't noticed before.

2. Thank you. Look at the left wall, and find something you haven't noticed before.

3. Thank you. Look at the right wall, and find something you haven't noticed before.

4. Thank you. Look at the back wall, and find something you haven't noticed before.

5. Thank you. Look at the ceiling, and find something you haven't noticed before.

6. Thank you. Look at the floor, and find something you haven't noticed before.

7. Thank you. Look at the front wall, and place your attention on the left wall.

8. Thank you. Look at the front wall, and place your attention on the back wall.

9. Thank you. Look at the front wall, and place your attention on the right wall.

10. Thank you. Look at the front wall, and place your attention on the ceiling.

11. Thank you. Look at the front wall, and place your attention on the floor.

12. Thank you. Look at the front wall, and place your attention on yourself.

13. Thank you. Look at the front wall, and place your attention on the sounds you hear.

14. Thank you. Look at the front wall, and place your attention on the bones in your body.

15. Thank you. Look at the front wall, and place your attention on the front wall.

16. Thank you. Decide in which direction you are going to look next.

17. Thank you. When you are sure you have decided, look in that direction.

18. Thank you. Decide in which direction you are going to look next.

19. Thank you. When you are sure you have decided, look in that direction.

exercise continues

20. Thank you. Decide in which direction you are going to look next.

21. Thank you. When you are sure you have decided, look in that direction.

22. Thank you. Decide in which direction you are going to look next and where you are going to place your attention.

23. Thank you. When you are sure you have decided, do it.

24. Thank you. Decide in which direction you are going to look next and where you are going to place your attention.

25. Thank you. When you are sure you have decided, do it.

26. Thank you. Decide in which direction you are going to look next and where you are going to place your attention.

27. Thank you. When you are sure you have decided, do it.

28. Thank you. Now with your eyes closed, put your attention on the right wall.

29. Thank you. Shift it to the left wall.

30. Thank you. Shift it back to the right wall.

31. Thank you. Shift it back to the left wall.

32. Thank you. Shift it to the back wall.

33. Thank you. Shift it to the front wall.

34. Thank you. Now divide your attention between the left wall and the right wall.

35. Thank you. Divide your attention between the front wall and the back wall.

36. Thank you. Divide your attention between the floor and the ceiling.

37. Thank you. Divide your attention between the floor and the ceiling and the front wall.

38. Thank you. Divide your attention between the floor and the ceiling and the front wall and the back wall.

39. Thank you. Divide your attention between the floor and the ceiling and the front wall and the back wall and the left wall.

40. Thank you. Divide your attention between the floor and the ceiling and the front wall and the back wall and the left wall and the right wall.

41. Thank you. Now reduce the effort you are using to place your attention on the floor, ceiling, front wall, back wall, left wall, and right wall.

42. Thank you. Okay, reduce the effort you are using even more.

43. Thank you. Once more, take the effort as low as it will go and still allow you to place your attention on the floor, ceiling, front wall, back wall, left wall, and right wall.

44. Thank you. Open your eyes, look around, and conclude this exercise.

Contemplation And Discussions

Contemplate means to study something carefully, to observe or imagine it from different angles and viewpoints. It is done repeatedly for a period of time in a two-stage process: first you place attention on the problem, question, or concept and then, after a few minutes, you relax and shift your attention to something else. Concentrating, relaxing, concentrating, relaxing, etc. Possibilities form and reform, progressing toward a moment of clarity in which you achieve insights and realizations.

Contemplation can take you beyond the familiar consciousness that you define as "mine" into several levels of impersonal consciousness culminating in the fabled "akashic record," depository of all life experience.

In similar fashion, group discussions explore an idea from different angles and viewpoints. When the participants are in alignment, a synergetic effect is created and the collective attention achieves insights and realizations.

Participants in group discussions should have the courage to express their ideas, should be tolerant of different viewpoints, and should listen in a manner that assists the evolvement of the answers being expressed.

Throughout the remainder of this workbook, there are questions posed for contemplation or discussion. Here is the first:

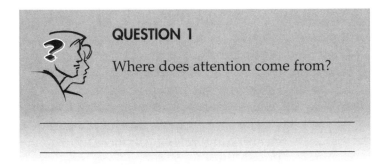

QUESTION 1

Where does attention come from?

_____

_____

Exploring a viewpoint.

Exercise 7

THE BEHAVIOR OF ATTENTION

When attention is not directed by the will, it behaves in response to the environment or according to past patterns.

OBJECTIVE:
To explore the behavior of attention.

Attention, like gravity, holds things in place by drawing them toward its source. The character of what is attracted is of no concern to either.

EXPECTED RESULTS:
Insights, improved well-being, recovery of self-determinism.

INSTRUCTIONS 1
For one minute, shift your attention around the room, and notice how it fixes for a few moments here or is repelled there. Most people can feel a difference between looking at their own hands or looking into a stranger's eyes. Attention lingers on certain things while other things push it away.

The surest way to make something persist is to resist it.

(If you're in a location that is very familiar to you, you may find that the attraction or repulsion force is nearly the same for everything. If so, redo the exercise in a space that is new to you, e.g., a shopping mall.)

INSTRUCTIONS 2

For one minute, close your eyes and review the events of the past week. Notice how your attention lingers on certain things while other things seem to push your attention away.

The Avatar Master Course, Noordwijkerhout, Holland

QUESTION 2

What determines the attraction-repulsion behavior of attention?

_____

_____

QUESTION 3

Think about something that you were once attracted to but are now repulsed by. What happened to cause that change?

_____

_____

QUESTION 4

Think about something that you were once repulsed by but are now attracted to. What happened to cause that change?

_____

_____

QUESTION 5

What causes attention to fix?

_____

_____

Exercise 8

EXHAUSTION OF ATTENTION

OBJECTIVE:

To deliberately create the experience of exhausted attention so that it may be identified when it occurs in your life.

EXPECTED RESULTS:

Temporary confusion, momentary unpleasantness, overwhelm.

(Caution: The use of this exercise is for demonstration only. If continued for longer than two or three minutes, it may produce an undesirable emotional state.)

INSTRUCTIONS

The following may be done in a group or by teaming up with another student. The group leader or coach reads quickly from the following list of instructions. The goal is to cause the participant(s) to experience exhaustion of attention.

1. Stand and face in a comfortable direction.

2. Once you have found your direction, stand on either your right or your left leg only, and elevate the opposite elbow to eye level.

3. Holding that position, make a fist with either hand, enclosing the thumb within the fingers, and hold the opposite hand, palm downward, fingers spread, at eye level.

4. While you do this, open your mouth, and place the tongue against the roof of your mouth.

5. While reversing the position left to right or right to left, maintain your balance and recite the alphabet backwards from the letter G.

Write a brief description of how you feel physically and emotionally when your attention approaches exhaustion.

NOTES

_____

_____

_____

_____

_____

_____

_____

_____

_____

_____

_____

Every identity (e.g., your name, definition, description, association, abilities, etc.) acts as a resistance to the flow of attention. When the resistance to attention exceeds the flow being directed by the will, you experience exhaustion, overwhelm, and confusion.

identity = *you + beliefs*

QUESTION 6

What is the relationship between environment and attention?

_____

_____

QUESTION 7

What is the relationship between attention and stress?

_____

_____

QUESTION 8

What is the relationship between attention and identity?

_____

_____

QUESTION 9

What is the relationship between attention and health?

_____

_____

QUESTION 10

What events, behaviors or relationships decrease your attention supply?

_____

_____

QUESTION 11

What events, behaviors or relationships increase your attention supply?

_____

_____

QUESTION 12

Why do the symptoms of chronic conditions show up when attention becomes exhausted?

_____

_____

How people habitually react to running out of attention determines their success in life. With this observation and using the attention exhaustion demonstration, an employer can quickly evaluate a potential employee's value or a potential participant can evaluate the success of any cooperative operation.

For example, when attention is exhausted:

• Sometimes people become victims; they react by asserting a disability as an excuse. They succeed by failing.

• Sometimes people give up; they react by criticizing the task. They seldom succeed.

• Sometimes people scheme and seek shortcuts; they react by rationalizing or altering procedures. To succeed, they need accurate instructions and constant supervision.

• Sometimes people become angry or irritable; they react by blaming or joking. To succeed, their responsibility needs to be clearly defined.

✪ Sometimes people acknowledge the overwhelm without taking it personally; they react by trying again. They succeed.

The best course of action for anyone to take when experiencing an exhaustion of attention is to compartmentalize the task into doable steps (prioritized lists) and to work on each step until it is complete or until it can be done correctly and with minimal attention drain. This is the value of practice.

Exercise 9

ATTENTION AND PRACTICE

OBJECTIVE:

To demonstrate the value of practice.

EXPECTED RESULTS:

Insights, improved well-being, recovery of attention.

INSTRUCTIONS

The following may be done in a group or by teaming up with another student. The group leader or coach reads a single line to the student, repeating each line as many times as necessary until the student is comfortable and able to perform each action without overwhelm, nervousness, or stress.

1. Stand and face in a comfortable direction.

2. Stand on either your right or your left leg only, and elevate the opposite elbow to eye level.

3. Holding that position, make a fist with either hand, enclosing the thumb within the fingers, and hold the opposite hand, palm downward, fingers spread, at eye level.

4. While you do this, open your mouth, and place the tongue against the roof of your mouth.

5. While reversing the above body position left to right or right to left, maintaining your balance, recite the alphabet backwards from the letter G.

The Wizard Course, Orlando, Florida

FREEING ATTENTION AND INSIGHT

Everything flows—eventually. When attention is alloyed with importance and judgments, it becomes emotional and sticks on things. It actually changes from a nonphysical wave form into very small physical particles that create thoughts with gravitational attraction. Certain ideas, objects, actions, or even areas can accumulate so many thoughts that they take on a life of their own. This is how identity is created. This is how amulets and ritual are created. This is how sacred ground is created. This is how the universe is created.

Some ideas, objects, actions, and areas are charged with great importance. The more importance assigned to something, the more attention it attracts. Attention directs attention. Stand on a street and look at the sky. Soon you'll have other people looking at the sky. Make something important enough, and it will consume a person's entire supply of attention. They will think about nothing else.

Some people, some events, some rituals are so charged with importance that they can cause a person to change viewpoints (or identity) and thus heal body parts, or even surrender self-control. This comes about by a very rapid shift of attention from one reality to a new reality. If the person who is shifted can sustain the shift (without attributing the phenomena to some external source), his or her life will stay changed: sudden conversion, spiritual healing, miracles.

Become good at shifting attention, build a few cathedrals, create a support group for your converts and...well, now you know. It is this knowledge that makes wizards popular in some circles and not in others.

Of course, if a person is operating with pure attention, this doesn't happen. Pure attention just observes, no emotional reaction. The person casually wonders what all the hubbub is about. Imagine Data or Spock from *Star Trek.* "Curious." That's a very Avatar attitude. "Interesting creation."

When a person's attention is nearing exhaustion, an inventory should be taken: What's really important here? What isn't really important here? With any luck there will be a few yawns and stretches as the importance and judgments separate from the attention particle, and it returns to its neutral, flowing energy form.

An interesting process for clarifying issues is to ask someone what's really important, and then help to focus ever finer by asking what's really important about that. This process will restore purpose to an organization and self-determinism to an individual.

As it turns out, the importance of any person, object, issue, event, or project is seldom an intrinsic aspect of the person, object, issue, event, or project, but is assigned by the observers and participants.

The Avatar Master Course, Bad Ems, Germany

Exercise 10

EMOTION AND IMPORTANCE

OBJECTIVE:

To determine the existing order of importance in your life.

EXPECTED RESULTS:

Insights, improved well-being, recovery of self-determinism.

INSTRUCTIONS

1. Make a list of ten people, objects, issues, events, or projects in which you have recently invested attention.

1. _____ ___ ___

2. _____ ___ ___

3. _____ ___ ___

4. _____ ___ ___

5. _____ ___ ___

6. _____ __ __

7. _____ __ __

8. _____ __ __

9. _____ __ __

10. _____ __ __

2. Assign each item in the above list an importance from 5 (very important) to 1 (not important at all).

3. Assign each item in the above list a judgment based on how closely it approaches the ideal you have of it: 5 (perfect) to 1 (not right at all).

SYN. **importance** the broadest of these terms, implies greatness of worth, meaning, influence, etc. (news of importance)

consequence often interchangeable with the preceding, more specifically suggests importance with regard to outcome or result (a disagreement of no consequence)

moment expresses this same idea of importance in effect with somewhat stronger force (affairs of great moment)

weight implies an estimation of the relative importance of something (his word carries great weight with us)

significance implies an importance or momentousness because of a special meaning that may or may not be immediately apparent (an event of significance)

Source: Webster's New World Dictionary

Here's a valuable little trick. When attention is being used to create something, it can get stuck on uncertainty. Directing attention through the uncertainty back to the result that you wish to create magically resolves the situation.

QUESTION 13

What effect does *alignment* or *misalignment* between your assignment of importance and your focus of attention have on your life?

_____

_____

The Avatar Master Course, Auckland, New Zealand

Exercise 11

MINDING THE EDGES

A long time ago, my mother taught me that the way to get through a horror movie without becoming too frightened was to "mind the edges" of the screen. *Minding the edges* means staying aware beyond the peripheral limits of the focus of your attention.

OBJECTIVE:

To learn to observe without attention becoming fixed.

EXPECTED RESULT:

The ability to shift attention.

INSTRUCTIONS

1. Take a walk and notice that your perceptual fields have edges (limits). Stay aware outside the limits.

2. Engage in a conversation with someone and mind the edges of what you see. Stay aware beyond the edges.

3. Recall a disturbing event, and mind the edges of the memory.

EX 1
EX 2
EX 3
EX 4
EX 5
EX 6
EX 7
EX 8
EX 9
EX 10
EX 11
EX 12
EX 13
EX 14
EX 15
EX 16
EX 17
EX 18
EX 19
EX 20
EX 21
EX 22
EX 23
EX 24
EX 25
EX 26
EX 27
EX 28
EX 29
EX 30

Exercise 12

RELEASING FIXED ATTENTION

Repeatedly extending attention into and retracting attention from an area where attention is fixed will eventually recover the fixed attention from that area. Usually the recovery happens abruptly and is accompanied by one or more of the following results:

- a sudden insight into the area

- the appearance of a solution

- the disappearance of the area altogether

- relief from pain

- discharge of an upset or an emotional release

- discharge of a past trauma

- a change in viewpoint (a reordering of importance)

Some areas may be so fixed or emotionally charged that you cannot immediately extend attention to them (unconscious memories) or retract attention from them (danger). These situations are addressed and remedied in the creation exercises of Section II Avatar materials.

OBJECTIVE:

To desensitize sensitive areas by removing fixed attention.

EXPECTED RESULTS:

Physical and emotional healing.

INSTRUCTIONS

Pick any sensitive area from the personality profile or from your life. Alternate between the following: 1) describe the area in detail until your attention is focused on it, then 2) describe something in your surroundings in detail until your attention is off the area. Repeat this process back and forth until one or more of the above results occurs.

Note: You should be prepared to run this process for extended lengths of time. It can open old wounds and should not be abandoned just because the going gets tough. You are tougher. See it through to conclusion.

The Avatar Master Course, Kyong Ju, Korea

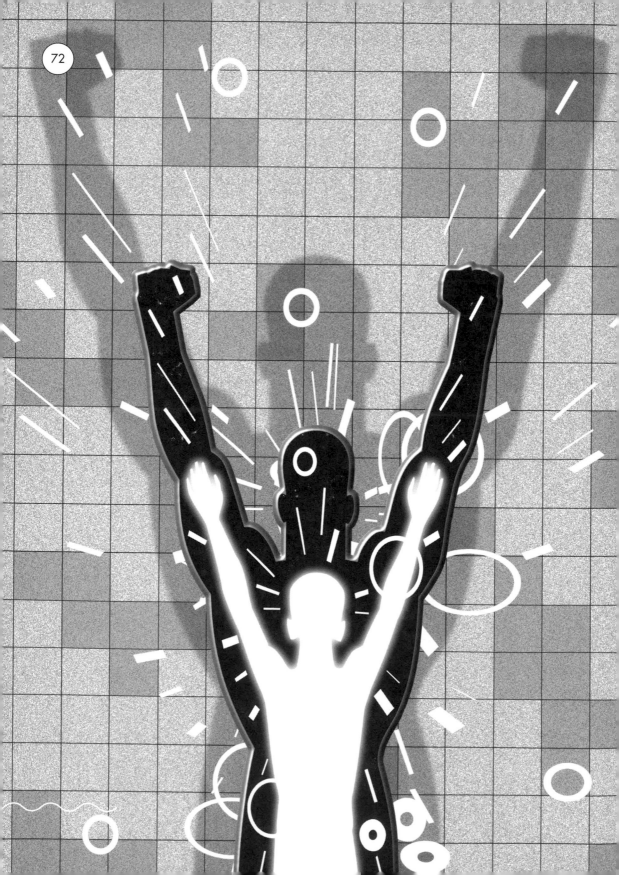

ATTENTION AND IDENTITY

Definitionless awareness is the source of attention. The more direct your connection, the purer your supply of attention. Compare the gaze of innocence in the eyes of a newborn to the averted, vacant stare of the derelict. Who is closer to definitionless awareness? Who has the greater attention? What has happened?

Pure beingness is egoless, compassionate, responsible, and totally nonjudgmental. Pure beingness is pure awareness.

When beings cease to be compassionate, responsible, and nonjudgmental toward creation, an interesting thing happens—they become creation! This is the Descent of Man.

The fall from innocence and grace begins with "I am this; I am not that." This statement is a denial of full responsibility and begins the process of defining yourself as something other than pure beingness. It is the beginning of duality. As soon as you say "This is what I am," you start being a conscious creation separate from "I am not that."

The more you deny responsibility, the more nouns you add after "I am." Consciousness has its roots in denial.

Gravity particles create mass.

Attention particles create self.

As you become more and more solidly defined, the window to definitionless awareness shrinks smaller and smaller. Living requires a flow of attention. The flow of attention must come from somewhere, so when you can no longer sustain life by an inward connection to source, you turn outward for the attention. This leads to pretense, courting displays, and people-pleasing behaviors. The pursuit of fame, wealth, and power ensue. Reputation, money, and influence are synthetic attention particles.

You feel starved for attention and begin borrowing heavily from others to sustain your creations. In place of the guileless, selfless "I" close to source, an ego-identity appears. Because the identity uses thought and emotion to attract attention, the attention it receives is highly alloyed with thought and emotion—more particles than waves.

As the ego-identity attracts particles of attention, it grows more and more solid. It calculates for the maximum attention advantage for its collection of particles. When attention cannot be attracted from others, it will be imagined. The imagination is a bypass conduit between the identity and source awareness. The identity can receive a sustaining flow of attention by imagining others who would, if present and informed, be fascinated by this or that accomplishment. Many lone-wolf types are actually sustaining their creations by acquiring attention through imaginary figures, e.g., comic-book heroes, fictional heroes, dead relatives, dead pets, defeated enemies, victimizers.

When attention cannot be inwardly sustained, attracted, or imagined, it will be demanded. This is the motivation behind premeditated antisocial behavior. Criminals are demanding attention particles. After exhausting the attention of their victims, they sabotage themselves into being caught to seek the attention of police, reporters, and judges. Without this mechanism at work, crime enforcement would be far less successful. (Ironically, the more attention paid to crime, the more criminals there will be. Vote for the first politician who truly understands this.)

If you eliminate psychological disorder at one end of the scale and selfless humanitarian acts at the other end, the middle ground will in one way or another be motivated by the attention market. The ego's sole purpose is to acquire attention from others, overtly or covertly. If it cannot coax attention, it will imagine it; if it cannot imagine it, it will demand it. This is the muddy game of life: emotional egos in competition, lost in fantasy or locked in conflict—costumed identities wrestling for attention.

Avatar is the path out.

Definitionless awareness is the source of attention.

Exercise 13

RESTORING ATTENTION

OBJECTIVE:
To collect your attention.

EXPECTED RESULTS:
Insights, improved well-being, recovery of self-determinism.

INSTRUCTIONS
Take a walk and count forms* until thinking diminishes or ceases entirely, and the world appears brighter.

*__form__ the shape, outline, or configuration of anything; structure as apart from color, material, etc.

EXAMPLE:
Look at a car, one; look at a leaf, two; look at a building, three; etc.

QUESTION 14
What is the relationship between satisfaction and attention?

_____

_____

ATTENTION AND BODY

The body is a creation and, like any other creation, attention is required to sustain it. The attention can be coaxed from outside sources, other life forms, even bacteria and viruses, or it can come through its connection with the spirits that inhabit it.

When the body fails to get nurturing attention, it will seek attention from injurious sources, and its general state of well-being will suffer. The purer the attention (compassionate, responsible, nonjudgmental), the more healthful it is to the body. Giving a body (your own or another's) the attention it needs by gentle massage, touching, grooming, etc., is health restoring. Giving it attention alloyed with criticism (thought) or sensual desire (emotion) can be damaging.

Attention alone should not replace competent medical treatment, but conversely, medical treatment without attention is seldom effective. A doctor's reassurance is often as good as the medicine prescribed.

If you wish to break a body-centered addiction, such as doing drugs, smoking, drinking, etc., the following exercise can be used to wean the body from its dependence on chemical attention.

Exercise 14

CARING FOR
THE ANIMAL

OBJECTIVE:

To handle craving for attention by the body.

EXPECTED RESULTS:

Improved well-being, relaxation, improved health.

INSTRUCTIONS

In private, secure, and comfortable surroundings, remove your clothing and spend fifteen minutes focusing your attention on your body. Pat it and stroke it. Talk to it. Treat it like a valued pet. The mood is nurturing and caring rather than sexual. Be forgiving and loving. Accept anything you consider a defect with the same compassion and understanding you would extend to another who possessed such a defect. Do not criticize or indulge in guilt. If you wish, you can apply a mud pack or a light body oil to the skin.

QUESTION 15

What is the relationship between habits and attention?

PART III

INTEGRITY

Exercises that may be done solo

Exercises that may be done with a companion

Exercises that may be done as a group

Questions for contemplation or group discussion

Refer to pages 83-88 of the book Living Deliberately.

BECOMING REAL

We are each born with a spark of divinity. When this spark glows brightly, we experience our best and noblest aspects. We cooperate and are real for each other. This condition occurs instinctively during times of crisis, but it can also be deliberately created to accomplish great works.

On the other hand, when the spark disappears we feel separation, and the egoistic and rapacious aspects of our natures appear. Custom and pretense replace realness in our relationships. Conflicts, quarrels, fear, and mistrust become commonplace.

What determines if our spark of divinity glows brightly, sharing its light and blessing with other divine sparks, or fades to black? Honesty. Honesty is the measure of our willingness for others to know our actions, our thoughts, our feelings, and our intentions. Anything that reduces this willingness separates us further from source.

When we are dishonest, we project onto those around us the actions, thoughts, feelings, and intentions that we are reluctant to express. They, the others, become the cheaters, swindlers, robbers, liars, or cowards that we will not admit in ourselves. We deny the worst by projecting it into the world where some broken soul, desperate for any attention, acts out our secret. Then we point an accusing finger and wash our hands of responsibility. We project onto the

honest *having a sense of honor; having honorable feelings, motives or principles; free from deceit or hypocrisy; true, candid, upright or just in speech and action; fair in dealing or sincere in utterance; worthy to be trusted*

integrate *to bring together into a whole*

integrity *unimpaired condition, wholeness, entireness, purity, completeness*

dishonest *having or exercising a disposition to deceive, cheat or defraud*

disintegrate *to separate into component parts; reduce to fragments; break up or destroy the cohesion of, as souls are disintegrated by a loss of honor*

honor *respect blended with some degree of reverence; esteem due to worth*

world our secret dishonesty, and it returns to us in the actions of strangers. Self-deception is the source of social decay in the world. Crime and violence have their beginnings in a denial of responsibility.

To protect our dishonesties from discovery, we shut ourselves off from the connection we have with other beings. Of course, we shut ourselves off from source as well. In place of honesty, there is pretense and identity. The door is closed. The cosmic gauge that measures wasted lifetimes creeps upward, but our innermost thoughts are safe. At such a cost! Imprisoned by our own secrets and numb to the pain we cause, we join the line of broken souls. No amount of punishment or humiliation is worse than the suffering we create for ourselves by being dishonest. If the world could only see.

But there is hope. If we drop the pretense and become really honest, something divine within us begins to awaken and grow. Balance is restored by a sincere effort to repair the damage that was done. We cease to deceive and begin to live deliberately. Freeing the attention fixed on our secrets empowers us to direct change and reshape lives. Habits and addictions that held us powerless become manageable; illnesses and upsets are healed; trusting relationships can be established—just by becoming honest.

The ability to accept and honor a trust, without enforcement or supervision, builds self-esteem.

*The solution is to begin to practice self-honesty
from where I am.*

*I will decide to exert my best efforts to become less
deceitful, to be more fair in my dealings,
more sincere in my speech, more deserving of
trust and MORE FORGIVING.*

*I can steer my own ship. I must! For if I am not
master of my course, I will never live in a world that
reflects real integrity.*

No one else can make the world honest.

Harry Palmer discusses viewpoints with Masters.

Exercise 15

WALK FOR ATONEMENT

This is a miraculous process. It works best up a mountain trail, a path through the woods, or up several flights of stairs. It can be done anywhere as long as each step is deliberate and accompanied by the prescribed confession. It can be done regarding your life in general or regarding a specific situation or regarding a specific person.

atonement *the reconciliation of a defined, contained, or limited consciousness with its source*

bless *to confer well-being or prosperity upon*

pretending *resisting what you really believe*

OBJECTIVE:
To relieve upsets and suffering.

EXPECTED RESULTS:
Relief from hostilities, upsets, and victimhood. New life.

INSTRUCTIONS
1. To begin your exercise you will need to pick a direction and a destination.

2. With each step toward your destination, whisper an action you have done or a thought or an intention you have had that was motivated by fear or anger. (Include any act you are reluctant to express or for which you feel guilt, any act for which you have a justifying belief or for which you feel a need to explain. Also include any non-actions when you really should have acted.)

3. At your destination, contemplate *spans of time.*

4. For each step you take on your return, think of someone and whisper the blessing, "May you be happy and well."

5. Release all thoughts and events to the past, and experience the sights, sounds, and sensations of the present moment with appreciation.

Variations of the Walk for Atonement Process

For self-abasement or self-abnegation:

- Use <u>self-criticisms</u> for instruction 2 and "I am happy and well" for instruction 4.

- Follow this exercise with <u>criticism of others</u> for instruction 2 and "okay" to something for instruction 4.

For being worried or troubled:

- Use <u>imagine something worse</u> (than the worry or trouble) for instruction 2 and "I am grateful for _____" for instruction 4.

For any period of time right before you made (or are about to make) a major change in your life:

- Use something you were <u>trying to keep secret</u> for instruction 2 and something you <u>could reveal</u> for instruction 4.

Exercise 16

SELF-DECEPTION SIGNALS

OBJECTIVE:
To learn to recognize the signals of self-deception.

EXPECTED RESULTS:
Insights, improved well-being, recovery of self-determinism.

INSTRUCTIONS:

A. List three errors that you frequently observe in others.

1. _____

2. _____

3. _____

QUESTION 16

Are there times you refuse to recognize these errors in yourself?

_____

_____

B. List three actions you engage in (or have engaged in) principally to persuade another to believe certain things about you.

1. _____

2. _____

3. _____

QUESTION 17

What beliefs are causing you to doubt these things about yourself?

_____

_____

C. List three conflicts in which you are involved.

1. _____

2. _____

3. _____

QUESTION 18

What beliefs are responsible for creating the circumstances of these struggles?

_____

_____

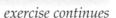

exercise continues

D. List three people (or groups, organizations, countries, etc.) you feel have abandoned you.

1. _____

2. _____

3. _____

Truth, should you ever wonder, is an alignment between what you are creating and what you are experiencing.

A lie is an attempt to experience something other than what you are creating.

Truth is the viewpoint of source.

A lie is basically an entertainment device.

QUESTION 19

What beliefs keep you from forgiving?

_____

_____

E. List three experiences that seem to happen repeatedly in your life.

1. _____

2. _____

3. _____

Here's a wake-up call: try creating right now exactly what you are experiencing right now.

QUESTION 20

What belief would someone have to have to create these experiences?

_____

_____

AVATAR LESSONS FOR A BETTER WORLD

1. When I am quick to find the error in others, I have failed to correct myself.

2. When my acts are designed to persuade another, I doubt myself.

3. When I experience struggle with the world, I have denied responsibility for my own creations.

4. When I feel separate and alone, I have failed to forgive.

5. When events repeat themselves in my life, there is a lesson I need to learn.

I can learn to be alert to my own self-deception. I can learn to recognize the signals that tell me I am losing my integrity.

Exercise 17

COMPASSION EXERCISE

Honesty with yourself leads to compassion for others.

Love is an expression of the willingness to create space in which something is allowed to change.

OBJECTIVE:
To increase the amount of compassion in the world.

EXPECTED RESULTS:
A personal sense of peace.

INSTRUCTIONS
This exercise can be done anywhere that people congregate (airports, malls, parks, beaches, etc.). It should be done on strangers, unobtrusively, from some distance. Try to do all five steps on the same person.

Step 1 With attention on the person, repeat to yourself: "Just like me, this person is seeking some happiness for his/her life."

Step 2 With attention on the person, repeat to yourself: "Just like me, this person is trying to avoid suffering in his/her life."

Step 3 With attention on the person, repeat to yourself: "Just like me, this person has known sadness, loneliness, and despair."

Step 4 With attention on the person, repeat to yourself: "Just like me, this person is seeking to
fulfill his/her needs."

Step 5 With attention on the person, repeat to yourself: "Just like me, this person is learning
about life."

Compassion Exercise Variations

1. To be done by couples and family
members to increase understanding
of each other.

2. To be done on old enemies and
antagonists still present in your
memories.

3. To be done on alien life forms.

PERSPECTIVE

The easiest way to change something is to change your viewpoint. This does not always result in a change in the world, but it will place you in the optimum position should you wish to make a change in the world.

The prize of experience is perspective; everything else is information.

• • • •

From the eternal stillness of source, you create each successive moment of existence, as it was, as it is, and as it will be. All joys, all sorrows, all opportunities and all limitations roll forth into creation from this stillness here now. Understanding that you are the convergent point of every reality is true perspective.

I have a self; I am the self.

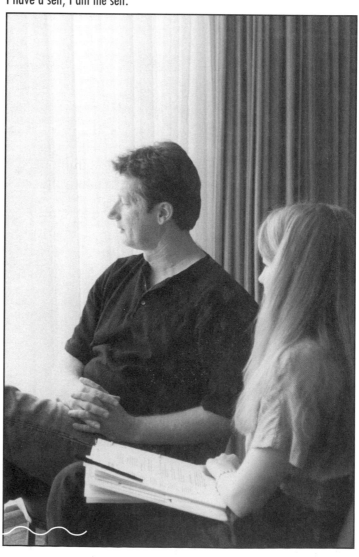

Exercise 18

VIEWPOINTS

OBJECTIVE:
To free attention.

EXPECTED RESULTS:
Increased calmness, broadened perspective.

INSTRUCTIONS
Take a thirty-minute walk. On your walk periodically notice something small; notice something big. Notice something far away; notice something close.

Write down any insights you gained from your walk.

standpoint *a position from which something is viewed*

viewpoint *a definition from which something is viewed*

awareness *a beyond from which everything is*

Exercise 19

THIS AND THAT

OBJECTIVE:
To demonstrate the effect of changing viewpoint.

EXPECTED RESULT:
Insights, increase in responsibility.

INSTRUCTIONS 1
Pick out something and think of it as *this* _____.

Pick out something and think of it as *that* _____.

Repeat with large and small objects, close and far objects, until you are confident of your ability to make anything this or that.

INSTRUCTIONS 2

Create each of the following first as *this (item)* and then as *that (same item)*:

(on your answers)	(on the concept)
your name	body
a pain	mind
an injury	self
a handicap	reality
a country	truth
	now
	here
	time
	world
	universe

Variation

For a powerful variation of the "This and That" exercise:

Do the list, first thinking of it as:
  I have (a)_____.
and then as
  I am (the)_____.

Exercise 20

CONVICTION

How much a belief affects reality is determined by the measure of certainty with which it is held. Conviction implies that doubts have been overcome.

OBJECTIVE:

To demonstrate the variable power of a belief.

EXPECTED RESULTS:

Insights into methodologies of indoctrination.

INSTRUCTIONS

Create your own scale of certainty extending from "extremely doubtful" at the bottom to "absolutely true" at the top.

For each step in your certainty scale, write at least one belief you have that falls at that level of certainty.

ABSOLUTELY TRUE

EXTREMELY DOUBTFUL

QUESTION 21

What changes the degree of certainty in a belief?

Never was there

anything outside of you,

never shall there be.

The infinite expressed,

a celebration to discover,

YOU are the ONE.

PART IV

You

Exercises that may be done solo

Exercises that may be done with a companion

Exercises that may be done as a group

Questions for contemplation or group discussion

BELIEFS

Consider the question: Are my beliefs shaped by my experiences, or do I experience what I believe?

If we consider those beliefs that arise as a result of our experience with the universe, e.g., because of so-and-so I believe, then we are talking about survival. We are talking about our ability to adapt to the way things are. This is defensive living.

But this leads to another question: Who created things the way they are? Now we're opening the stage to hungry gods—gods who have nothing better to do than to test man, seducer gods who bait their traps with temptation and create creatures who struggle to resist. Is this reasonable or is there another possibility? Perhaps we create things the way they are, descend into our own creations, and then forget the way home.

The penalty for accepting the viewpoint that our experience with the world is the source of our beliefs is that we become creatures burdened with limitation and surrounded by challenges to survive.

So there we are, scurrying around trying to decide which consequences are going to kill us and what we might do to survive a while longer. Then without warning, some bodhisattva, an Avatar, walks through our lives and reshapes reality by such pure acts of faith that somewhere deep inside it all, in a place behind who we thought we were, a new "I" awakens.

Things look different from that place, clearer, less threatening. The attitude changes from sufferer to explorer. We start to make connections, to see patterns.

Are my experiences affected by what I believe? At first people are suspicious of such questions. Somehow they reshuffle the deck. It seems too easy. Then curiosity causes them to look a little closer.

You experience what you believe, unless you believe you won't, in which case you don't, which means you did.

Yes, believing certain things creates standards against which they evaluate experience. That's true; they believe in certain moral values. This is good and that is bad. And yes, sometimes moral values change, and it is possible that people could then enjoy some things that they don't enjoy now. Of course, this is just idle speculation.

But it does seem that how you experience the universe may have as much to do with what you believe as it has to do with what is happening.

Exercise 21

OPERATING BELIEFS

OBJECTIVE:

To determine if the beliefs you hold are helpful or harmful.

EXPECTED RESULTS:

Insights, restructuring of personal reality.

INSTRUCTIONS

List three things you believe about yourself.

1. _____

2. _____

3. _____

List three things you believe about relationships.

1. _____

2. _____

3. _____

exercise continues

EX 1
EX 2
EX 3
EX 4
EX 5
EX 6
EX 7
EX 8
EX 9
EX 10
EX 11
EX 12
EX 13
EX 14
EX 15
EX 16
EX 17
EX 18
EX 19
EX 20
EX 21
EX 22
EX 23
EX 24
EX 25
EX 26
EX 27
EX 28
EX 29
EX 30

List three things you believe about money.

1 _____

2. _____

3. _____

List three things you believe about governments.

1 _____

2. _____

3. _____

List three things you believe about work.

1 _____

2. _____

3. _____

List three things you believe about your ability.

1 _____

2. _____

3. _____

List three things you believe about your health.

1_____

2. _____

3. _____

List three things you believe about your family.

1_____

2. _____

3. _____

List three things you believe about the future.

1_____

2. _____

3. _____

a. After each belief you wrote, note whether you experience the belief as helpful (H) or impeding (I).

b. After each belief you wrote, note the degree of certainty (from the scale you created in Exercise 20) that you place in it.

exercise continues

c. Finally, after each belief you wrote, note whether the belief was assumed deliberately (DEL) or was indoctrinated into you (IND).

• • • •

What conclusions can you draw after doing a, b, and c above?

_____

_____

_____

_____

_____

_____

_____

_____

_____

_____

_____

Exercise 22

BELIEF AND
INDOCTRINATION

Viewpoints are composed of beliefs. It's easier to observe what people believe than it is to have them tell you. People who say they believe one thing yet experience something different are saying what they believe they ought to believe rather than what they do believe.

OBJECTIVE:

To explore the cause-and-effect relationship between beliefs and experiences.

EXPECTED RESULTS:

Insights, increase in personal responsibility.

INSTRUCTIONS

List what someone else ought to believe.

1_____

2. _____

3. _____

exercise continues

4 _____

5. _____

6. _____

QUESTION 22

What is the relationship between
what you believe and what you
think others ought to believe?

_____

_____

Exercise 23

TRANSPARENT BELIEFS

A belief is transparent when you are operating through the belief without noticing it. Transparent beliefs are seldom helpful and, in fact, can be fatally debilitating. Most are self-sabotaging, adopted in a moment when you were something less than rational.

The first impression you have of a transparent belief is that it is unquestionably true. That's just the way life is. That's the way I am. Here's the proof! But then something funny happens: you discover that the proof for holding the belief is actually produced by the belief itself. A pattern begins to unfold.

Transparent beliefs are discovered by tricking yourself into expressing them and then stepping back and looking at what you said. Transparent beliefs are often hidden under the desire to be right, so finding transparent beliefs requires a degree of vulnerability.

OBJECTIVE:

To discover transparent beliefs.

EXPECTED RESULTS:

Insights, personal transformation.

exercise continues

INSTRUCTIONS

Discovering transparent beliefs is done either with a companion or as a team effort. The exercise may be repeated many times.

Step 1 The guide or group leader asks, "What would you like to change?" until a situation is revealed.

Step 2 Once the situation has been pinpointed, the guide or group leader goes after:

- the beliefs that are creating the situation

- the experiences that are reinforcing the beliefs, i.e., creating certainty in the beliefs

by asking:

(a) What belief might someone have in order to experience (situation)?

(b) How do you prove that belief is true?

(c) What other belief might someone have in order to experience (situation)?

(d) How do you prove that belief is true?

(c) and (d) are alternately addressed until the student has a realization.

Example of a Transparent Belief Session

GUIDE	STUDENT
What would you like to change?	My fear of talking to people I don't know.
(a) What belief might someone have in order to experience a fear of talking to people he doesn't know?	People might say something bad.
(b) How do you prove that belief is true?	I've got examples. I've seen it happen. I've done it.
(c) What other belief might someone have in order to experience a fear of talking to people he doesn't know?	I might say something stupid.
(d) How do you prove that belief is true?	I said something really stupid to my friend's wife.
(c) What other belief might someone have in order to experience a fear of talking to people he doesn't know?	Don't talk to strangers. It's good advice for children. Aha! I just realized something. It's not because I don't know them that I don't talk to them. It's because they don't know me! I'm the stranger. The belief is— strangers are dangerous.

Personal reality reflects what a person really believes—not always the same as what he/she may be pretending to believe.

When people do not act deliberately, transparent beliefs govern their lives.

(Note: Some sessions last considerably longer than this example.)

TALKING ABOUT ~~AWARENESS~~ CONSCIOUSNESS

As soon as we talk about awareness it becomes consciousness. And as we talk about consciousness, we assume a viewpoint. And when that viewpoint fixes, it becomes part of an identity.

To confuse matters more, any of these—awareness, consciousness, viewpoint or identity—answers to "you" and operates as "I."

Awareness is the ultimate shape-shifter. It will conform itself to any belief system imposed upon it. The more conviction, the more conformity. Once it is defined, it can be studied in elaborate, scholarly detail and will create a thoroughly real, measurable experience. But it will never reveal anything more profound than the fact that it is conforming to a belief system being imposed upon it. Proving something true/false is a descent into consciousness.

The edges of consciousness are coincident with your extension of attention in time and space.

The mantra of awareness is not Om; it is Aaah!

So why not impose something more interesting on awareness than a dutiful repeat of the past? Live deliberately! Extricating "I" from the habits of the past is not an easy trick, but fortunately you have Avatar to do this. Let's start with self-defining beliefs that create packages called identities. Identities determine what is most readily perceived and how it is interpreted. Identity is what keeps transparent beliefs transparent.

Some identities conflict with each other, and some identities reinforce each other.

Most people have different identities that are changed from time to time like suits of clothes. One identity is employed to make sense of things at work, another identity is assumed to relate to the family, and a third identity functions as a student. Sometimes the identities are changed deliberately—as in the moment you take to gather yourself before meeting a new date or a customer—and other identities change automatically in response to events or people. Come on; let's go exploring.

As soon as we talk about awareness it becomes consciousness.

Exercise 24

EXPLORING DEFINITION

OBJECTIVE:
To explore the definitions that you are currently imposing on awareness.

EXPECTED RESULTS:
Insights, relief from fixed conditions.

Be in the present moment; then be the present moment. Be in the here; then be the here.

INSTRUCTIONS
In response to the stimulus in parentheses, fill in the following with spontaneous answers.

1. (Health) I am _____

2. (Nationality) I am _____

3. (Profession) I am _____

4. (Ability) I am _____

5. (Financially) I am _____

6. (Size) I am _____

exercise continues

7. (Attitude) I am _____

8. (Status) I am _____

9. (Education) I am _____

10. (Reputation) I am _____

11. (Sex) I am _____

12. (Sexual preference) I am _____

13. (Relationship) I am _____

14. (Integrity) I am _____

15. (Courage) I am _____

16. (Perseverance) I am _____

17. (Ambition) I am _____

18. (Pride) I am _____

19. (Sensitivity) I am _____

20. (Blame) I am _____

21. (Loyalty) I am _____

22. (Deservedly) I am _____

23. (Fortune) I am _____

24. (Of necessity) I am _____

Don't let what you're being get in the way of what you might become.

Exercise 25

MOTIVATION

Three ways in which you come to define yourself are:

1) by deliberately modeling

2) by resistance to an antagonistic person or opinion

3) by obedience to someone's expectation

OBJECTIVE:

To discover the motivation(s) behind various self-definitions.

EXPECTED RESULTS:

Insights, relief, redefinition.

INSTRUCTIONS

For each definition you wrote in Exercise 24, determine if the item was motivated by:

1) modeling

2) resistance

3) obedience

Note: A full handling of identity (and the conditions associated with identities) is found in Section III of the Avatar materials.

EX 25

Exercise 26

EXPANSION EXERCISE

The process of ceasing to identify yourself with a location or definition and gradually assuming the beingness of a larger whole is called integration.

Consider when you feel the flesh of your hand. Do you feel each cell that makes up your hand, or do you feel an integrated sensation of the entire hand?

What if you were able to relocate the boundaries of the location or the definition you consider you?

Do you end at the skin? Or do you extend beyond? What do you believe?

OBJECTIVE:

To convey an experience of expansion and integration.

EXPECTED RESULTS:

Insights, reconciliation.

INSTRUCTIONS

The following is done as a guided meditation. (For best results, precede this exercise by a few minutes of the "This and That" exercise on page 96.)

• Get some impression of the space you occupy. (pause)

• How far out does it extend? (pause)

- As effortlessly as you can, make your space extend in all directions. (pause)

- Include everyone and everything. (pause)

- Now get the impression that you contain the space you have just created. (pause)

- Feel where you come from. (pause)

   (Go through entire meditation three times.)

QUESTION 23

Where do you come from?
(And before that?)

_____

_____

Brush the
dust off
your dreams.

LIVING DELIBERATELY

Personal alignment means to be in agreement with and to work toward some goal.

When people are uncertain of their direction or goals, they tend to act in a misaligned fashion. They wander around, one step forward, one step backward, and generally get in their own way. In order to accomplish anything, they need continuous outside direction: *Here, do this. Go this way.*

Personal misalignment comes from having uncertain or conflicting goals.

Most people have learned that it's important to set goals, but few recognize that *there are right and wrong goals, as well as proper and improper ways to set goals.*

Some people have multiple goals that are misaligned or in contradiction with each other. They want to go to the movie, but they don't want to go by themselves. They want to have relationships and families, but they don't want to sacrifice anything. They want to earn money, but they don't want to work. They want to lose weight, but they don't want to give up eating high calorie foods. They want to go to school, but they don't want to study. People who are misaligned create confusion in their lives. The confusion becomes so overwhelming that they end up doing nothing. The result of misalignment is limited achievement, limited success, poor health, and unhappiness.

As a step toward living deliberately, you should decide on your life goals. Granted, these may change as you progress up the line, but the experience gained from setting and pursuing the goal is the real prize.

Picking a goal is not an arbitrary thing. It is not done by the flip of a coin or by an opportunistic turn of events. It is not done to please another person.

What goals make your life worth living?

Setting a Right-For-You Goal (RFY goal) is done by using your best reasoning liberally seasoned with your intuition. It is reasonable, because you sincerely feel you can achieve it. It is intuitive, because it feels right. An RFY goal excites you when you think about it. It empowers you. It brings you to life. It sizzles! It provides you with the creative energy for its own attainment plus a little extra.

Just imagining what it would feel like to achieve the RFY goal will tap into the courage and determination to accomplish it.

If you wonder if your chosen goals are RFY goals, notice how you feel when you pursue them. Activity spent in the pursuit of an RFY goal is enjoyable and absorbing. Time is forgotten. Work is pleasurable. The pursuit of an RFY goal is its own reward.

A non-RFY goal is something you "have to" do while waiting to get to what you want to do. You become exhausted and time drags. Work is grueling. The payoff for pursuing a non-RFY goal is stress.

Exercise 27

GOAL SETTING

OBJECTIVE:
To determine a Right-For-You Goal

EXPECTED RESULT:
A life plan that you can begin to follow deliberately.

INSTRUCTIONS
STEP 1

On a clean sheet of paper, make a list of goals. This list contains goals you are already pursuing or have thought about pursuing or that are stimulated by the following questions:

1. What do you want to achieve in the next year?

2. What do you want to own by the end of next year?

3. What would you like to do by the end of next year?

4. What excites you most?

5. What would you have to become to do what you want?

6. Where would you like to be in two years?

7. Where would you like to be in five years?

8. Where would you like to be in ten years?

9. Where would you like to be in twenty years?

exercise continues

10. Where would you like to be in fifty years?

11. Where would you like to be in one hundred years?

12. Where would you like to be in one thousand years?

13. What goals have you given up on?

14. What would you really like to do?

15. If you knew you couldn't fail, what would you attempt?

16. When are you happiest?

17. What do the people you most admire do?

18. What were your goals when you were younger?

19. What would you like to do just for the heck of it?

20. What do you consider to be too late to start on?

21. If it weren't for _____, what would you do?

22. What might not be impossible?

STEP 2

On your list, rate the goals you are most interested in according to the following seven criteria:

Rate: (1) very doubtful to (5) very certain.

1. The goal invites your attention and interest. Thinking about it renews your strength.

| | 1 | 2 | 3 | 4 | 5 |

2. Pursuit of the goal produces something of value to you.

| | 1 | 2 | 3 | 4 | 5 |

3. The goal offers benefits to others equal to your own.

    1   2   3   4   5

4. The goal presents an opportunity for self development (greater competence, understanding, or responsibility).

    1   2   3   4   5

5. The goal is in alignment with a broader group goal and a still broader humankind goal.

    1   2   3   4   5

6. The goal allows personal creativity and some degree of self management.

    1   2   3   4   5

7. The goal presents the opportunity for personal recognition and some receipt of others' admiration.

    1   2   3   4   5

Add the total score for each goal (35 is a perfect score).

If a goal scores between 25 and 35, it's probably an RFY goal. If you have several goals that scored between 25 and 35, see if you can come up with a larger, more expansive goal that encompasses and aligns all your RFY goals.

If you had only goals that scored between 15 and 25, see if you can modify one of the goals to score higher.

If all your goals scored below 15, you should take a walk and then repeat this exercise.

Exercise 28

LIFE ALIGNMENT PROGRAM

OBJECTIVE:
To begin to align your attention and energy with the goal you wish to achieve.

EXPECTED RESULTS:
The recognition that there is a path to success.

alignment an adjustment of energies, ideas, or intentions toward a personal or a collective goal

INSTRUCTIONS
Determining your goal or goals is the first step. The next step is to align your life and actions toward the goal.

STEP 1
Make a list of your weekly activities.

_____

_____

_____

_____

_____

After each of the activities, note whether the activity is helpful (H) to you or impeding (I) to you.

STEP 2

Make a list of your major expenses.

_____

_____

_____

_____

_____

After each of the expenses, note whether the expense is helpful (H) to you or impeding (I) to you.

STEP 3

Make a list of your beliefs regarding this goal.

_____

_____

_____

_____

_____

After each of the beliefs, note whether the belief is helpful (H) to you or impeding (I) to you.

Exercise 29

CREATE YOUR
OWN EPITAPH

Defining consciousness is an activity engaged in by a being between the portals of birth and death. It is assumed that awareness itself passes these portals, waking from its shells of definition as it goes.

OBJECTIVE:
To remind you of what a profound experience life is.

EXPECTED RESULT:
Increased perspective.

Understanding that you create your own reality, you learn to experience it as devoutly and as respectfully as any blessing bestowed by any Infinite Creator.

INSTRUCTIONS
Write an honest epitaph in tribute to your life thus far.

_____

_____

_____

_____

_____

_____

_____

DEBRIEFING

Debriefing is an alignment technique. It is an oral or written response to three questions:

1) What did you set out to do (i.e., what was your purpose, mission, intention)?

2) What did you actually do?

3) What actually happened?

The value of a debrief is that, in clarifying your intention and actions and their results, you are not relying on someone else's evaluation of your performance (job, project, task, etc.) and will realize whether or not the exercise is complete, correctly done, or appropriate for what you are attempting to accomplish. If your intention in doing an exercise is to remove an emotional block and what actually happens is that you are still blocked, then the exercise is either incomplete or done incorrectly or inappropriate for what you are trying to accomplish.

If you are doing *ReSurfacing* by yourself, you can judge the appropriateness of an exercise by determining if it is producing insight, emotional change, or viewpoint shift. If you are working with an Avatar Master (or trainer), your debrief will quickly inform him or her of how you are doing.

Awareness Koan:

Two things that are exactly
the same in all aspects —
are they not the same thing?

Exercise 30

DEBRIEF

On Your Study Of Section I Avatar

OBJECTIVE:

The following debriefing questions will provide feedback to Star's Edge on the effectiveness of this workbook.

EXPECTED RESULTS:

Free attention.

INSTRUCTIONS

What did you set out to do?_____

_____

_____

What did you actually do? _____

_____

_____

What actually happened? _____

_____

_____

Please mail or fax to:

Quality Control
Star's Edge International
237 N. Westmonte Drive
Altamonte Springs, FL
32714
USA

FAX (407) 788-1052

(optional)
Name:

Address:

CHECK ONE:
○ *Mission accomplished* ○ *Mission incomplete*
○ *Actions inappropriate*

Quality Control
Star's Edge International
237 N Westmonte Dr
Altamonte Springs, Florida 32714
USA

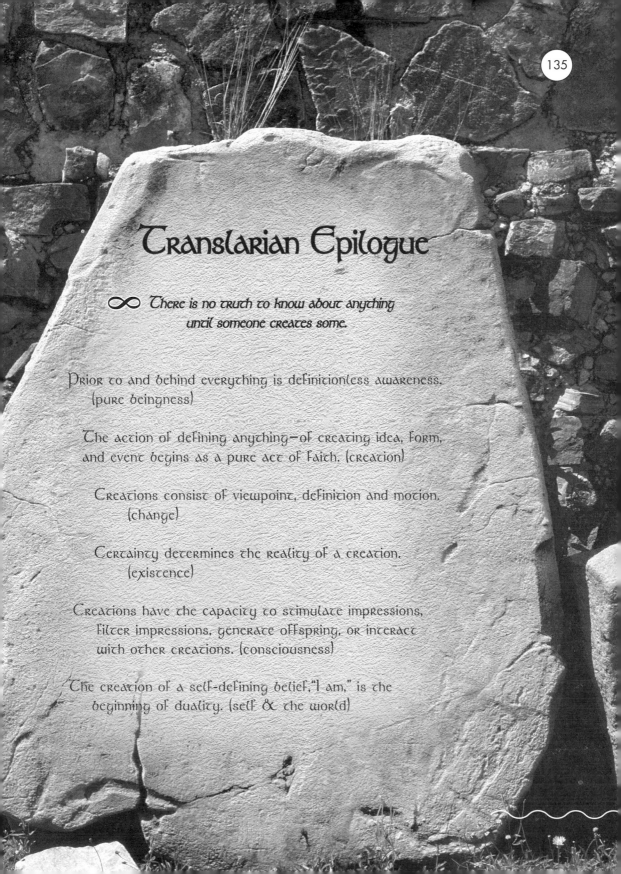

Translarian Epilogue

∞ *There is no truth to know about anything
until someone creates some.*

Prior to and behind everything is definitionless awareness.
(pure beingness)

The action of defining anything—of creating idea, form,
and event begins as a pure act of faith. (creation)

Creations consist of viewpoint, definition and motion.
(change)

Certainty determines the reality of a creation.
(existence)

Creations have the capacity to stimulate impressions,
filter impressions, generate offspring, or interact
with other creations. (consciousness)

The creation of a self-defining belief, "I am," is the
beginning of duality. (self & the world)

Within the defined limits of any "I," the action of defining anything—of creating idea, form, and event—begins by believing. (mind)

Within the defined limits of any "I," creations have the capacity to stimulate impressions, filter impressions, generate offspring, or interact with other creations. (thought)

Within the defined limits of any creation, creations have the capacity to...other creations.

Creations can be changed by their creators. (free will)

New viewpoint changes viewpoint. (experience)

New definition changes definition. (decision)

New motion changes motion. (action)

Perception is composed of impressions, generated by creations, that interact with other creations. (sensation)

Understanding is composed of beliefs through which perceptions are interpreted as meaningful. (knowledge)

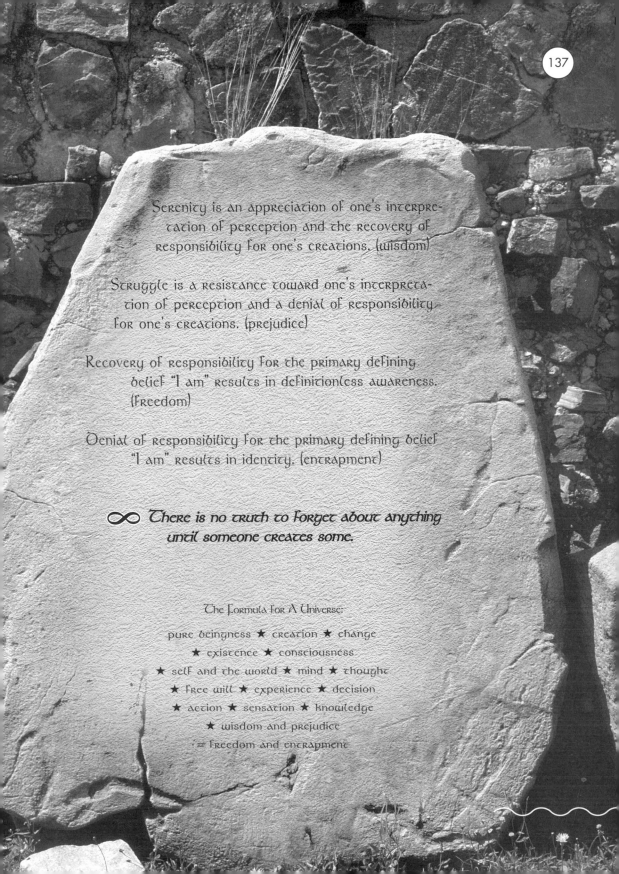

Serenity is an appreciation of one's interpretation of perception and the recovery of responsibility for one's creations. (wisdom)

Struggle is a resistance toward one's interpretation of perception and a denial of responsibility for one's creations. (prejudice)

Recovery of responsibility for the primary defining belief "I am" results in definitionless awareness. (freedom)

Denial of responsibility for the primary defining belief "I am" results in identity. (entrapment)

∞ There is no truth to forget about anything until someone creates some.

The Formula for A Universe:

pure beingness ★ creation ★ change
★ existence ★ consciousness
★ self and the world ★ mind ★ thought
★ free will ★ experience ★ decision
★ action ★ sensation ★ knowledge
★ wisdom and prejudice
= freedom and entrapment

PART V

THE NEXT STEP

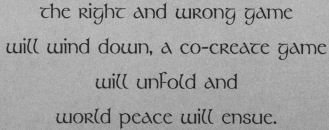

The mission of Avatar
in the world is to catalyze the
integration of belief systems.

When we perceive that
the only difference between us is our
beliefs and that beliefs can be created or
discreated with ease,
the right and wrong game
will wind down, a co-create game
will unfold and
world peace will ensue.

SECTIONS II & III OF THE AVATAR COURSE

Sections II and III of The Avatar Course are neither long nor complex, yet they introduce techniques that can have an even greater liberating effect on human consciousness than the exercises of *ReSurfacing.* Your Avatar Master will guide you into exploring realms wherein you can deliberately modify both personal reality and collective reality. This training, as you will soon see, is a breakthrough in the creation of human ability. All exercises and initiations are supervised by Avatar Masters trained and licensed to deliver Avatar by Star's Edge, Inc.

The two study packs, *Section II, The Creation Exercises,* and *Section III, The Avatar Rundowns,* are confidential and are provided for your study by the Master. Sections II and III study packs remain the property of the Master and may not be distributed or sold. In large centers where many people are working together, students will be required to sign out their study packs when they enroll or when they review the courses.

Sections II and III are confidential so that the materials may be presented in a systematic manner that will allow them to be utilized fully. Reading, intellectualizing, or even believing in the materials will not create an Avatar. A well-trained and disciplined Master is required to ensure that the Avatar techniques make it off the page and into your life. Sections II and III become valuable and verifiable

The truth that an Avatar Master teaches does not require a name, for it does not pass through the world, but is the loving model of willingness to share consciousness.

only when they are conveyed by a Master. Properly presented, they attune you to your own unique world lessons, which in the final analysis are what really create the Avatar. Life, understood, is the teacher.

You will be provided with a personal folder that contains additional materials and is used to store your write-ups, lists, and summaries. The personal folder also contains the course checklist, which lists the sequence in which the materials are to be studied and the exercises and programs are to be done. Each item on the checklist is completed to your satisfaction and then initialed off by you with time and date.

The checklist will help both you and the Master keep track of progress. Checked-off items may be reviewed by the students, and on occasion, may be reassigned by the Master. (Good Masters are caring and unreasonably insistent that you achieve the expected results.)

Am I...?

Sometimes a person may wonder if he has reached the end of the self-development trail and has already obtained the results that Sections II and III of Avatar offer.

There is an easy test.

Would you have any resistance to creating exactly what you are experiencing?

If you have any reluctance about answering "no," there is still a ways to go.

STAR'S EDGE PHILOSOPHY

Star's Edge International is the corporation that manages the delivery and expansion of Avatar. It was founded in 1986 to oversee and manage the secular affairs associated with creating an enlightened planetary civilization.

Some individuals have wondered why Star's Edge does not operate as a nonprofit institute and teach Avatar on the basis of goodwill donations. They argue that the Avatar materials are far too important to remain the proprietary property of any individual or company. There is some merit to their argument, but the flaw—and it is a fatal one—is the assumption that the existing society will act in its own behalf to preserve and spread this new technology. Historically, technologies not associated with profit are short-lived.

Introducing a new technology to an established civilization requires that somebody do something more than say, "Here it is. Take it. Give me what you think it is worth." Somebody has to ensure that the technology is purely presented and not biased toward someone's belief system or slanted to support someone's personal motivation. Somebody has to manage the hundreds of variables and decision points that inevitably arise in cooperative acts of this size. Somebody has to think ahead. Somebody has to deal with vested interests. Somebody has to settle disputes and keep everything on track. Somebody has to pay the bills.

Avatar, managed properly, is a catalyst to accelerate the creation of an enlightened global civilization that can be entrusted with the responsible custodianship of this planet. It is that important. It *is* that important!

When you adopt the viewpoint that there is nothing that exists that is not part of you, that there is no one who exists who is not part of you, that any judgment you make is self-judgment, that any criticism you level is self-criticism, you will wisely extend to yourself an unconditional love that will be the light of your world.

The Avatar program is a straightforward exchange of a valuable training program for valuable financial consideration. When you understand how really clean this is, and the ramifications, you will realize how refreshing and certain of success is our approach to creating an enlightened planetary civilization.

We're not founding a new religious sect or any sort of true faith zealots. We don't want to convey any belief system or series of agreements to people. We do not have a hidden agenda, nor do we apologize for being prosperous and powerful. Whoever created the belief that poverty and world service go hand-in-hand cost humanity the help of some of the brightest people who have ever lived.

Any prospective student may write, call, or fax Star's Edge International to determine the current licensing status of any Master.

Our intention is that the people we train and license to deliver Avatar charge money (not worship nor homage nor admiration, but currency alone) for their valuable service and that they charge enough to guarantee that Avatar continues to expand and attract the able. We intend to set an example for the world: *prosperity and good works belong together.*

Avatar, properly presented, is the most powerful, purest self-development program available at any price. It is the shared responsibility of Star's Edge, Avatar Masters, and every Avatar student to insist this standard of quality be maintained. We play a big game.

Internally, the Star's Edge organization operates with three hearts: ♥ that of the companion, which is a loving heart characterized by *sharing, friendship, and cooperation;* ♥ that of the guide, which is a caring heart characterized by *patience, compassion, and reason;* and ♥ that of the guardian, which is a fierce heart characterized by *integrity, courage, and justice.*

THE PATH OF AVATAR

THE PATH OF AVATAR®

Avatar® Course	Requirements	Available From
Section I Checklist or *ReSurfacing®* Workshop	None	Any Master currently licensed to deliver Avatar
Section II The Exercises	A familiarity with *ReSurfacing®*	Any Master currently licensed to deliver Avatar
Section III The Rundowns	Recovery of the experience of your own sourceness	Any Master currently licensed to deliver Avatar

Master™ Course	Requirements	Available From
Section IV (a) Awakening	Completion of The Avatar Course and an invitation from your Master.	Delivered only by Star's Edge delivery teams
Section IV (b) Beyond Awakening	Delivery of The Avatar Course	Delivered only by Star's Edge delivery teams

Wizard™ Course	Requirements	Available From
Section V Extrasensory abilities	Completion of Section IV (a) of The Master Course	Delivered only by Star's Edge International

Teaches About	Expected Results	1998 Cost/Time
Preliminary course information. Philosophical principles of Avatar. Exercises to produce insight and connection with higher levels of consciousness.	Greater connection with and insight into the nature of personal reality. The ability to discover your secret-most beliefs.	Checklist: US$100 1 day or Workshop: US$295 2 days
The principles governing creation and experience. Exercises to enhance the perception of creation and to restore the ability to create reality.	The ability to perceive reality without judgments, distortion or separation; to modify personal reality; to create experientially real states of beingness at will.	US$500 4 to 5 days
The principles governing discreation and the management of reality. Personal initiation and seven solo rundowns that handle aspects of existence.	The ability to change body sensations, interpersonal conflicts, dependencies, self-sabotaging beliefs, and compulsions; to assume full responsibility for the conditions and circumstances of your own life.	US$1500 2 to 4 days

Teaches About	Expected Results	1998 Cost/Time
Source Beingness. The structure and mechanics of personal identity. Locating core beliefs. Shifting perspective. Instructions on delivering initiation sessions and supervising rundowns.	The ability to handle persistent conditions. A certainty on the workability of the Avatar materials. A one-year provisional license to organize and conduct Avatar deliveries that achieve the expected results.	US$3000 9 days
The components of life: Beingness, Motivation, Perception, Operation, Organization, Alignment. Using attention to create without becoming trapped by it.	An understanding of the purpose of life and the ability to remain comfortably present in difficult circumstances.	US$2500 7 days

Teaches About	Expected Results	1998 Cost/Time
The collective consciousness. Levels and abilities of consciousness. Hidden influences on life. Leadership and civilization management.	The ability to understand and manage creation. The ability to operate from the viewpoint of the higher self. The ability to transform civilization.	US$7500 13 days

PART VI

INDEX

ALIGNMENT

WHO AM I?
WHY AM I HERE?
WHERE AM I GOING?

Hear the personal breakthroughs of other students (some as they actually occur).

ReSurfacing is a new approach to these age-old questions. You find the answers by exploring the underlying structure of your own consciousness. It's easier than you might think.

Personalize your expedition into consciousness to fit your own needs. How far you go is a matter for you to determine. There is no effort to indoctrinate you with someone else's belief or truth. What you believe is what you believe, and the truth you discover is your truth.

Enjoy original music (including Burton Cumming's "One Day Soon" and the Hottracks hit, "Simple As That").

With the *ReSurfacing Audio Workshop* you are able to proceed through the exercises at your own pace. You are part of an actual ReSurfacing class. Listen and compare your fellow students' views to the actual experiences you explore with the exercises. You will be amazed.

The ReSurfacing Audio Workshop:

- Six cassette tapes (over 4 hours of instructions, discussions and surprises)
- Audio Workshop manual with 30 exercises including your own personality profile
- A $50 coupon toward a LIVE ReSurfacing workshop or The Avatar Course
- Information to access the rapidly expanding world of Avatar, including a free one-year subscription to the worldwide *Avatar Journal*
- A chart of the services and expected results of the Avatar path

Act now to begin the adventure of a lifetime.

Star's Edge International
237 North Westmonte Drive
Altamonte Springs, Florida 32714
tel: 407-788-3090 • 800-589-3767
fax: 407-788-1052
e-mail: avatar@avatarhq.com

The ReSurfacing Audio Workshop includes a **$50 coupon** toward a *Live* ReSurfacing Workshop or The Avatar Course.

"When I started, my mind was so busy that I couldn't turn it off. After the exercise, I grew quiet and my energy level soared."

"I used the Minding the Edges exercise to help our family through the experience of my brother's death."

"The Counting Forms exercise is a good way of waking up to the world. It leaves you in a more expansive space."

"Doing the Compassion Exercise at work took care of some interpersonal difficulties that had existed for a long time."

The ReSurfacing Audio Workshop is $49.95 U.S. and can be ordered with a credit card by calling 800-589-3767 or 407-788-3090.

Living Deliberately:

THE DISCOVERY AND DEVELOPMENT OF AVATAR

In 1987, an educational psychologist named Harry Palmer outlined an intriguing series of mental procedures. When correctly applied, these procedures unravel many of the more profound mysteries of human consciousness.

Living Deliberately is $15 U.S. and can be ordered with a credit card by calling 800-589-3767 or 407-788-3090.

For the first time, a clear interrelation between the operation of human awareness and the technologies of man could be demonstrated. Subjects as dissimilar as religion and physics suddenly found themselves sharing common ground. Concepts such as universal mind, mass consciousness, and extrasensory awareness moved from being dim and speculative to being tangibly experiential.

Living Deliberately is an autobiographical account of Harry's search for a better way—for enlightenment—which ultimately led to the discovery and development of The Avatar Materials.